United States
Department of
Agriculture

Forest Service

**Northern
Research Station**

General Technical
Report NRS-5

Historical Perspective on the Reintroduction of the Fisher and American Marten in Wisconsin and Michigan

Bronwyn W. Williams
Jonathan H. Gilbert
Patrick A. Zollner

Abstract

Management of mustelid species such as fishers and martens requires an understanding of the history of local populations. This is particularly true in areas where populations were extirpated and restored through reintroduction efforts. During the late 19th and 20th centuries, fishers (*Martes pennanti*) and American martens (*Martes americana*) were extirpated from much of their southern range, including Michigan and Wisconsin. Both species have been restored to varying degrees in these states following multiple reintroductions and translocations. We describe the status of the original populations and changes in their status over time, and include source locations, release sites, release and reintroduction dates, and demographic characteristics of released animals. This synthesis is crucial for evaluating the relative success of reintroductions in Michigan and Wisconsin, and, combined with knowledge of the current condition of these populations, can provide valuable guidance on the future management of these species. We also assess the reintroduction of fishers and martens in Michigan and Wisconsin and discuss strategies for successful reintroductions.

The Authors

BRONWYN W. WILLIAMS is a graduate student with the University of Alberta, Department of Biological Sciences, Edmonton, Alberta, Canada. JONATHAN H. GILBERT is a wildlife biologist with the Great Lakes Indian Fish and Wildlife Commission, Odanah, WI. PATRICK A. ZOLLNER, formerly a research ecologist with the North Central Research Station at Rhinelander, Wisconsin, is an assistant professor with Purdue University, Department of Forestry and Natural Resources, West Lafayette, IN.

Cover Art with permission from Gabriela Sincich, Museum of Latin American Art, Long Beach, CA.

INTRODUCTION

Knowledge of the history of local populations is critical to the management and conservation of most species, particularly when reintroductions have been made or are planned. Fishers (*Martes pennanti*) and martens (*Martes americana*) are frequently reintroduced species (Berg 1982), and populations in Michigan and Wisconsin provide unique opportunities to examine the effects of multiple reintroductions into areas where both species were extirpated (e.g., Williams 2006). Detailed stocking records, including source, numbers and sex ratios released, and location of releases, can be used to test theoretical predictions related to founder events, and assist in design, application, and assessment of management decisions, including reintroductions in the Midwest and other areas.

HISTORICAL DISTRIBUTION OF FISHERS IN NORTH AMERICA

The fisher is an exclusively North American species. The northern limit of the fisher's former range was the lower Iskut area of British Columbia near the Alaska border (Macleod 1950), across the southeastern corner of the Yukon Territory (Rand 1944), south of the Liard River and Resolution in the Northwest Territories (Richardson 1829), and south of a line connecting the southern tip of James Bay and Mingan, Quebec (Bell 1884; Fig. 1). Fishers were found along the Cascade and Sierra-Nevada Mountains (Baird 1859; Rhoads 1898; Grinnell et al. 1937), in Wyoming and the Northern Rocky Mountains (Skinner 1927; Cahalane 1947), into the southern Great Lakes States (Plummer 1844; Kennicott 1855; Brayton 1882), and the Appalachian Mountains into Tennessee, Virginia, and North Carolina (Audubon and Bachman 1851-1854; Allen 1876; Rhoads 1896; Kellogg 1937).

Changes in Historical Distribution

Extensive logging and multiple fires throughout the 19th and early 20th centuries degraded forested habitat occupied by fishers. High prices for fisher pelts increased harvest pressure on this easily trapped species (Cook and Hamilton 1957). In 1920, prime pelts sold for as much as $300 (Brander and Books 1973).

Harvest records suggested a severe decrease in the numbers of fishers across the southern portion of the species' range. In Wisconsin, 559 fishers were taken during the 1917-18 trapping season. Three years later, only three fishers were trapped (Brander and Books 1973). Similarly in California, 102 fishers were taken in 1920 and two fishers were trapped in 1931 (Brander and Books 1973). In response to observed declines in harvest, trapping seasons for fishers were closed in 1922 in Wisconsin, 1924 in Michigan, 1929 in Minnesota, 1935 in New Hampshire, 1936 in New York and Wyoming, 1937 in Maine and Oregon, and 1946 in California (Brander and Books 1973; Sodders 1999).

Trapping bans and the recovery of habitat allowed fisher populations to recover in some states. For example, fishers had been nearly trapped to extinction in New York by the 1930s but a closed harvest season from 1936 to 1949 corresponded to a population increase (Bradle 1957; Irvine et al. 1964). By 1949, the number of fishers in New York was deemed sufficient to allow a limited trapping season. In 1957, the season bag limit was increased to three fishers per person (Bradle 1957).

Minnesota also retained a remnant fisher population following protection of the species in 1928. Increased numbers of fishers allowed for a limited intrastate

Figure 1.—Approximation of historic and recent distribution of fishers in North America; adapted from Hagmeier (1956), Powell (1993), Gibilisco (1994), and unpublished state agency reports.

translocation of 15 animals from the northeastern to the northwestern portion of the State (Itasca State Park) in 1968 (Berg 1982). A trapping season was initiated in 1977-78, with a bag limit of three fishers per person (Berg 1982).

Natural recolonization and a number of reintroduction attempts (e.g., Benson 1959; Weckwerth and Wright 1968; Fuller 1975; Pack and Cromer 1981; Berg 1982) resulted in the recovery of fishers in some areas of their historical range (e.g., across Eastern North America and Montana). Conversely, fisher populations remain absent or fragmented south of the Great Lakes and in the Pacific Northwest (Harris et al. 1982; Zielinski et al. 1995; Fig. 1).

HISTORY OF FISHERS IN WISCONSIN AND MICHIGAN

Pre-reintroduction Status

Fishers reportedly were found throughout Wisconsin but the last verified sighting was in 1932 (Hagmeier 1956; Hine et al. 1975; Petersen et al. 1977). In Michigan, fishers had been found as far south as Gratiot, Ingham, Washtenaw, Wayne, and Wexford Counties in the Lower Peninsula (Burt 1948). The last confirmed sighting was in 1936 in Marquette County, Upper Peninsula (Sodders 1999).

The Fisher and the Porcupine

Changes in forest cover from harvest and fires in addition to the decrease and eventual extirpation of the fisher from much of its southern range were followed by an apparent increase in the number of porcupines (*Erethizon dorsatum*) in those areas. The increase in porcupine populations and associated forest damage spurred managers to initiate control activities. In the Ottawa National Forest (ONF), Upper Peninsula, Michigan, estimated porcupine densities were as high as 23 per km^2 by the late 1950s (Brander and Brooks 1973). In 1961, 1,799 porcupines were shot on the ONF. Road hunts that same year yielded an average of one porcupine shot per 2.9 km (Irvine 1961).

Porcupines were associated with timber loss due to their feeding habits. A 1948-49 study conducted on the Argonne Experimental Forest in Wisconsin showed that hardwood-hemlock forests sustained serious damage with 24.5 or more porcupines per km^2. An intensive harvest during this study resulted in 37 porcupines killed per km^2 (Irvine and Brander 1971). There was major concern in the 1950s that unchecked population growth of porcupines could result in substantial timber losses (Olson 1966).

Fishers are purportedly efficient predators of porcupines (Schoonmaker 1938; Earle 1978). Reports of increasing numbers of fishers in the Adirondack Mountains of New York and in northeastern Minnesota paralleled reports of decreasing porcupine numbers (Olson 1966). The inferred causation was mostly a matter of speculation as no controlled studies had been conducted to determine whether fishers alone could control porcupine populations (Irvine and Brander 1971). However, conjecture that fishers could control the species that apparently was creating economic turmoil in the timber industry sparked interest in restocking the mustelid to Michigan and Wisconsin (Olson 1966; USDA For. Serv. interoffice commun.).

Reintroduction and Translocation of Fishers in Wisconsin and Michigan

Reintroductions

The Forest Service first proposed reintroducing the fisher as a biological control of porcupines in 1955 (Olson 1966). A conservation rationale was concurrently proposed by A.W. Schorger, former Wisconsin

Conservation Commissioner, who was interested in restoring extirpated wildlife species to Wisconsin. Dr. Antoon de Vos of the Ontario Department of Lands and Forests, known for his work with fishers in Canada, was invited to assess the quality of the habitat in northern Wisconsin for possible reintroduction of the fisher (Olson 1966).

By the 1950s, the price of fisher pelts was sufficiently low that the illegal trapping of this animal appeared to be limited (Cook and Hamilton 1957). The fashion industry had created much of the high demand for fishers, and a shift in women's fur fashions to spotted cats resulted in a decline in the price of fisher pelts from as high as $300 to $5 to $15 (Brander and Books 1973).

Shortly following a "favorable" assessment by Dr. de Vos, the Wisconsin Conservation Department (currently the Wisconsin Department of Natural Resources, WDNR) began negotiations with New York State to acquire fishers for a reintroduction (Irvine et al. 1964). The steady growth of the fisher population in the Adirondack Mountains presented an opportunity for the New York Conservation Department to trade fishers to Wisconsin for bobwhite quail (Bradle 1957; Irvine et al. 1964). During the winter of 1955-56, seven fishers from the southern fringe of the Adirondack Mountains were shipped to Wisconsin and were released in the Argonne District of the Nicolet National Forest (NNF). Seven additional fishers in three separate shipments from New York were released on the NNF during the winter of 1956-57 (Bradle 1957) and four animals were released in 1958. The total number included 12 females and six males (Petersen et al. 1977; Table 1, Fig. 2).

Following the initial fisher reintroductions, a 16,187-ha closed area, the Nicolet Fisher Management Unit (NFMU), was established around the release sites (Bradle 1957; Irvine et al. 1964). Harvest and dry-set trapping was prohibited in the closed area because fishers often were caught incidentally in baited traps set for other animals (Olson 1966).

The NFMU was located in the Pine River watershed and was dominated by dense hardwoods and large

Table 1.—Demographic data of reintroductions of fishers in Michigan and Wisconsin

Release location	Date	N (females)	Source population
1. Nicolet National Forest, Fisher Management Unit, Forest County, WI	1956	7 ⎤	Adirondack Mountains, New York
	1957	7 ⎢ 18 (12)	Adirondack Mountains, New York
	1958	4 ⎦	Adirondack Mountains, New York
	1958	3 ⎤	Superior National Forest, Minnesota
		⎢ 12 (3)	
	1959	9 ⎦	Superior National Forest, Minnesota
	1962	26 (9)	Superior National Forest, Minnesota
	1963	4 (0)	Superior National Forest, Minnesota
	Total: 1956-1963	60 (24)	
2. Ottawa National Forest, MI	1961	31 (8)	
Tomlin Hill: T48N R37W Section 20	1962	16 (5)	
Ottawa National Forest, MI	1963	14 (6)	
	Total: 1961-1963	61 (19)	Superior National Forest, Minnesota
3. Chequamegon National Forest, Fisher Management Unit, Bayfield and Ashland Cos., WI	1966	31 (13)	
	1967	29 (17)	
	Total: 1966-1967	60 (30)	Superior National Forest, Minnesota

coniferous swamps (Bradle 1957; Irvine et al. 1964). In 1962, NFMU, renamed the Fisher/Marten Closed Area (FMCA), was enlarged to 48,562 ha. To discourage the incidental taking of dispersing fishers in dry-set traps, state bounty payments on furbearer species such as bobcats and coyotes in Wisconsin were discontinued in 1963 (Olson 1966), though county bounty payments remained in effect until 1980 (Hubert 1982).

Following initiation of fisher restocking in Wisconsin, the Forest Service arranged with the Minnesota Department of Conservation to live-trap fishers on the Superior National Forest (SNF). These animals would continue the reintroduction on the NNF and additional individuals would be stocked on the ONF, which is immediately north and northwest of the NNF (Irvine

et al. 1964). Three and nine fishers trapped on the SNF were released on the NFMU in 1958 and 1959, respectively, including nine males and three females. In 1962, 26 fishers (nine females and 17 males) from the SNF were released on the NFMU. Finally, four males were released on the NNF in 1963. From 1956 to 1963, 60 fishers (24 females and 36 males) were released on the NFMU-FMCA (Petersen et al. 1977; Table 1, Fig. 2).

In 1961, 31 fishers (eight females and 23 males) trapped on the SNF were released on the ONF. In January and February of 1962, an additional 16 fishers (five females and 11 males) were released north of Kenton, Michigan, at Tomlin Hill, approximately 29 km north of the 1961 release site. Eighteen fishers had been trapped on the SNF for the second stocking, but one male and one

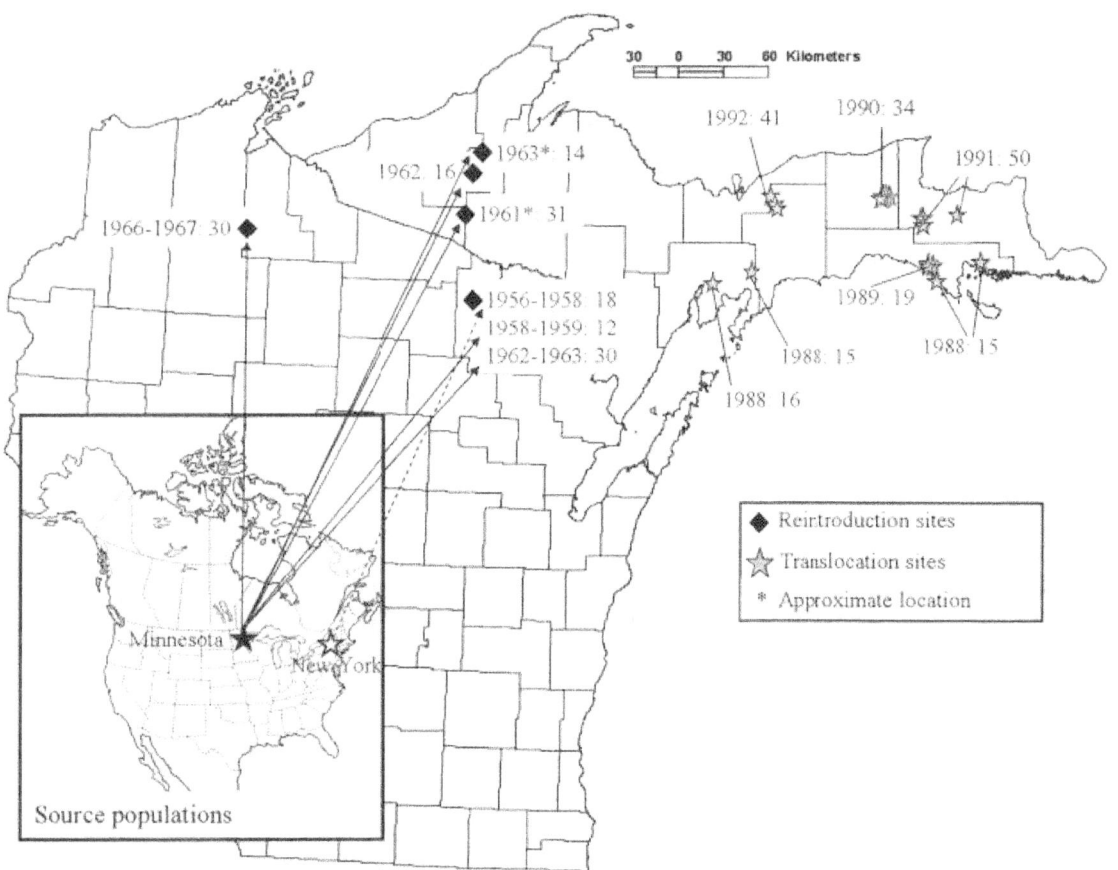

Figure 2.—Locations of fisher reintroductions and subsequent translocations in Wisconsin and Michigan, 1956-92.

female died prior to release (Irvine 1962). The third and final release of 14 fishers (six females and eight males) was in 1963. From 1961 to 1963, 61 fishers (19 females and 42 males) were released on the ONF (Irvine 1962; Berg 1982; Table 1, Fig. 2). To discourage trapping methods that would incidentally capture fishers in and around the ONF, all bounty payments except those on coyotes were eliminated by 1965 (Olson 1966; Hubert 1982).

The release of fishers on the NNF and ONF was suspected to be the cause of a decrease in the number of porcupines in those areas. In 1971, porcupine populations in two localized areas on the ONF were 25 and 55 percent of the total recorded in 1962 (Irvine and Brander 1971). Although silvicultural practices (R. Brander, USDA Forest Service retired, personal commun.) or forest successional changes might have reduced the amount of preferred porcupine habitat and thus species abundance, the speculated relationship

between fishers and porcupines prompted the release of 60 fishers (30 females and 30 males) on the Chequamegon National Forest (CNF) in Wisconsin in 1966 and 1967. In 1966, 31 fishers (13 females and 18 males) from the SNF were released on the CNF followed by a release of 29 fishers (17 females and 12 males) in 1967 (Table 1, Fig. 2). A second Wisconsin fisher management area was established on the CNF (CFMU) on 48,562 ha surrounding the release site in Bayfield and Ashland Counties. As on the NFMU, fisher harvest and dry-set trapping was prohibited on the CFMU (Petersen et al. 1977).

Translocations

By the 1980s, fishers had colonized most of Michigan's western Upper Peninsula. It was thought that natural dispersal eastward had been halted by a band of agricultural land and thus a lack of suitable habitat bisecting the Upper Peninsula (Mich. Dep. Nat. Resour.

Table 2.—Demographic data of translocations of fishers in Michigan

Release location		Date	N (females)	Source population
1. Rapid River Dist., Hiawatha NF, West Unit		1988	16 (11)	
Manistique Dist., Hiawatha NF, West Unit		1988	15 (10)	
St. Ignace Dist., Hiawatha NF, East Unit		1988	15 (6)	
	Total:	*1988*	*46 (27)*	Iron, Gogebic, Ontonagon, Baraga, Houghton Counties, MI
2. Mackinac County		*1989*	*19 (8)*	Iron, Baraga Counties, MI
3. Luce County		*1990*	*34 (19)*	Iron, Baraga Counties, MI
4. Chippewa County		*1991*	*50 (25)*	Ontonagon, Houghton, Baraga Counties, MI
5. Schoolcraft and Mackinac Counties		*1992*	*41 (22)[a]*	Iron, Baraga, Houghton, Ontonagon Counties, MI

[a] Forty-one fishers were trapped, but only 40 released; final sex ratio is unknown.

1990). The boundary of this dispersal barrier followed a north-south line from 16 km east of Marquette to 16 km west of Escanaba.[1]

One goal of the fisher reintroduction in Michigan was to restore an extirpated species to its former range given the existence of suitable habitat. The long-term goal was to provide Michigan residents with the opportunity to enjoy the fisher from an aesthetic, ecological, recreation, and economic perspective.[1] To attain both goals and overcome the perceived barrier to natural dispersal in the central Upper Peninsula, a 5-year translocation plan was developed to encourage colonization of fishers in the eastern Upper Peninsula.

In February and March of 1988, 46 fishers (27 females and 19 males) were trapped in portions of Iron, Gogebic, Ontonagon, Baraga, and Houghton Counties. The trapping area was bordered by State Route 45 on the west, State Route 28 on the north, U.S. 141 on the east, and the Wisconsin border on the south, according to the Michigan Department of Natural Resources (MDNR) (unpublished). Fifteen fishers (six females and nine males) were released on the St. Ignace District, East Unit of the Hiawatha National Forest (HNF) in Mackinac

County. Thirty-one animals were released on the West unit of the HNF in Delta County (Rapid River District: 11 females and five males; Manistique District: 10 females and five males) (Steck 1988; Table 2, Fig. 3).

In February and March 1989, 19 fishers (eight females and 11 males) were trapped in portions of Iron and Baraga Counties, Michigan, and released in Mackinac County (Steck 1989; Table 2, Fig. 3). During January and February of 1990, 34 fishers (19 females and 15 males) trapped in portions of Iron and Baraga Counties were released in Luce County (Steck 1990; Table 2, Fig. 3). In February 1991, 52 fishers were trapped in portions of Ontonagon, Houghton, and Baraga Counties and 50 (25 females and 25 males) were released in Chippewa County (MDNR unpublished; Table 2, Fig. 3). One trapped animal was albino and released at the trapping site after much publicity. Another individual escaped while being transferred to the release site (MDNR unpublished).

In 1992, 41 fishers (22 females and 19 males) were captured in portions of Iron, Baraga, Houghton, and Ontonagon Counties for the final translocation. Forty animals were relocated, including 37 individuals released in Schoolcraft County and three released in Mackinac County (MDNR interoffice commun.; Table 2, Fig. 3).

[1]Wagner, D., Fisher plan (unpublished). Mich. Dep. Nat. Resour., Wildl. Div.

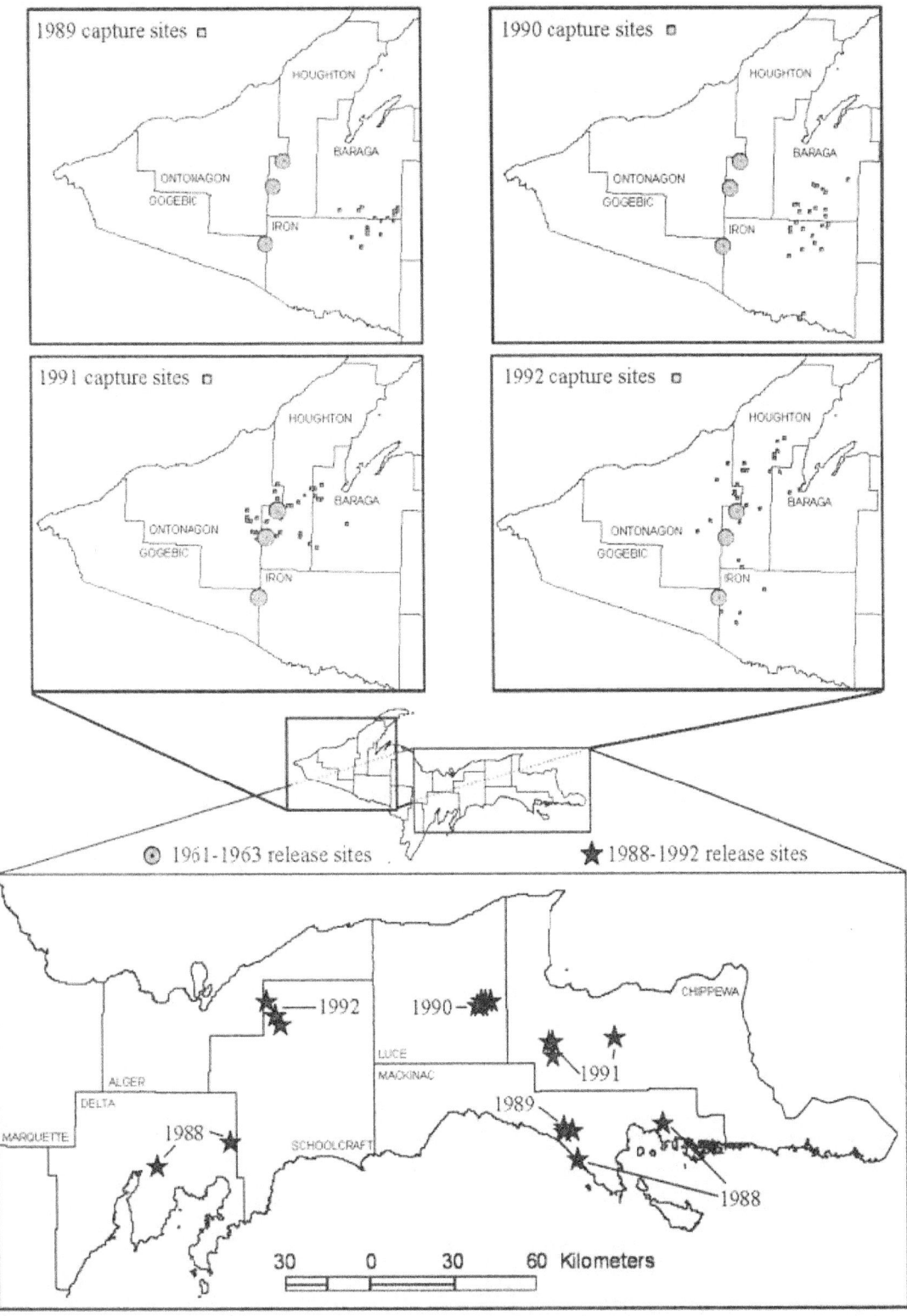

Figure 3.—Trapping locations (section of capture) in the Western Upper Peninsula and release locations in the Eastern Upper Peninsula of the 1989-92 translocated fishers.

STATUS OF FISHERS IN WISCONSIN AND MICHIGAN

Fishers have colonized most areas across Wisconsin and the Upper Peninsula of Michigan. The first modern trapping season in Wisconsin was established in 1985 (Dhuey et al. 2000). The current population estimate is 11,700 fishers (R. Rolley, WDNR, pers. commun.). Fishers have been reported as far south as Manitowoc County and are also found in Door County, a peninsula that projects into Lake Michigan from east-central Wisconsin (Davis 1997). The current range of fishers across northern Wisconsin may have resulted from natural dispersal from Minnesota in addition to dispersal from the release sites on the CNF and NNF.

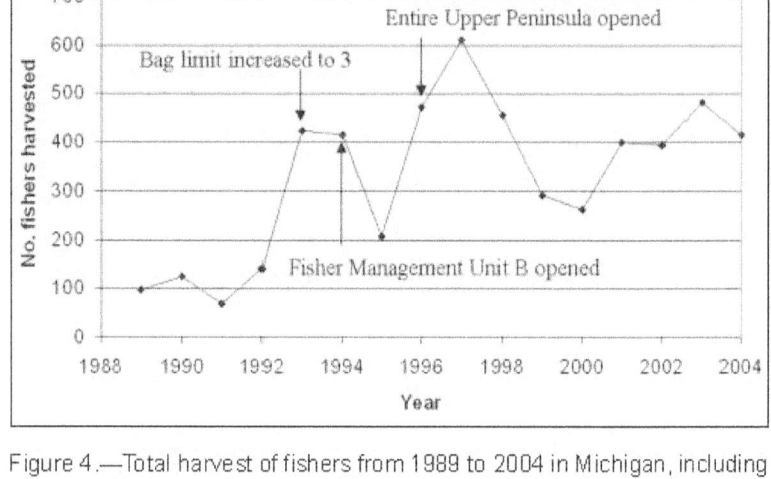

Figure 4.—Total harvest of fishers from 1989 to 2004 in Michigan, including years in which management decisions were made regarding quotas and areas trapped.

In Michigan, the first legal fisher harvest season in 60 years was established in 1989 (Cooley et al. 1990). Since that time, there has been a general increase in the number of harvested fishers (Cooley et al. 1990, 1991, 1992, 1993, 1994, 1995, 1997a, b, 1998, 2001; M. Cosgrove, MDNR, pers. commun.; Fig. 4). Spatial distribution of harvest locations from 1989 to 2004 indicates the presence of fishers across most of the Upper Peninsula (Fig. 5).

HISTORICAL DISTRIBUTION OF AMERICAN MARTENS IN NORTH AMERICA

The historical range of the American marten was coincident with the distribution of the northern coniferous forests (Hagmeier 1956; Gibilisco 1994). The northern boundary of the species' range was from northern Alaska, across northern Yukon Territory and Northwest Territories, and through northern Manitoba, Ontario, and Quebec (Hagmeier 1956; Fig. 6). The southern portion of this range included the mountains along the Pacific Coast (Grinnell et al. 1937), the Wasatch, Yellowstone, and Uinta areas of the Rocky Mountains in Wyoming and Utah (Seton 1925-28; Hagmeier 1956), throughout high elevations (> 2,900 m) in Colorado, to northern New Mexico (Bailey 1931; Williams 1947; Fig. 6). Martens also were found in the

northern Great Lakes States (Schorger 1942), across northern Pennsylvania (Rhoads 1903), northward through the Berkshire Mountains of Massachusetts (Emmons 1840), Green Mountains of Vermont (Kirk 1916), White Mountains of New Hampshire (Allen 1904), into northern Maine (Seton 1925-28; Fig. 6).

In addition to coniferous habitats, martens are found in hardwoods, particularly mixed deciduous-coniferous forests that sustain substantial populations of prey species (e.g., de Vos 1951). Much of the marten's distribution has been sympatric with that of the larger fisher, resulting in the potential for interference competition. In areas with substantial differences in elevation, such as in the West or Northeast, martens generally are found at higher elevations than fishers (Hagmeier 1956). Snow depth seems to limit the sympatry of the two species, with smaller, lighter martens with furred feet able to maneuver more efficiently through deep snow (Raine 1983; Aubry and Houston 1992; Krohn et al. 1995; Krohn et al. 1997).

Changes in Historical Distribution

The same pressures affecting fishers in the 19th and early 20th centuries also led to a rapid decline in the number of martens across the southern portion of its range and in the Midwest. Marten habitat (mature forests) was

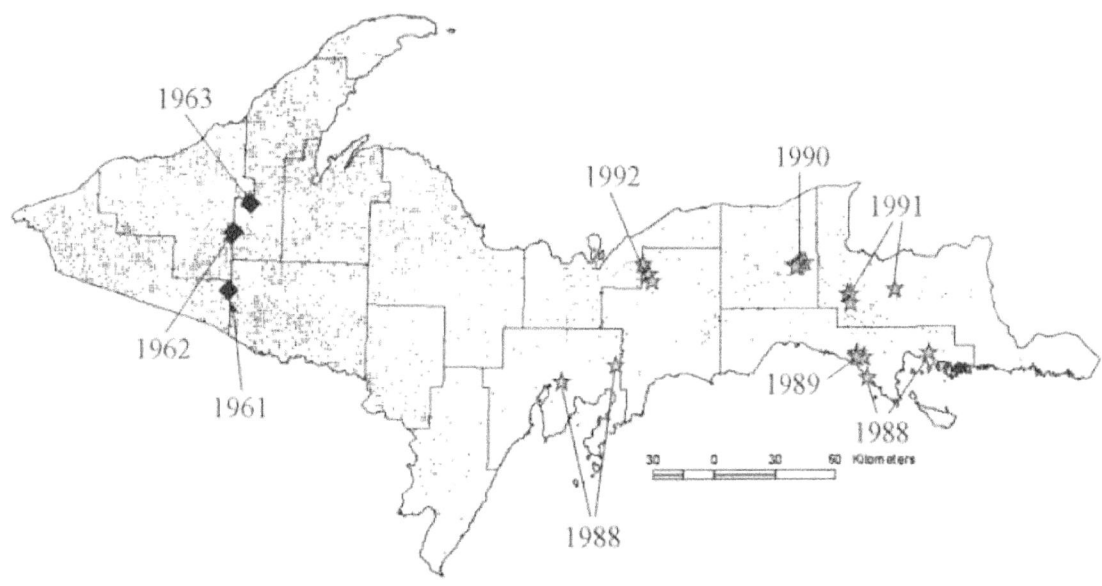

Figure 5.—Location of reported harvested fishers in the Upper Peninsula of Michigan from 1989 to 2004 (release locations are provided for reference).

Figure 6.—Approximation of historic and current distribution of American martens in North America; adapted from Hagmeier (1956), Gibilisco (1994), and unpublished reports by the Michigan Department of Natural Resources and Wisconsin Department of Natural Resources.

Table 3.—Demographic data of reintroductions of martens in Apostle Island National Lakeshore, Wisconsin

Release location	Date	N (females)	Source population
Apostle Island National Lakeshore, Stockton Island, Ashland Co.	1953	5 (Unknown)	Near Kalispell, Montana

degraded by logging and fires, and high prices for marten pelts along with unregulated trapping severely depleted populations of this animal (Berg 1982).

By the early 1940s, marten abundance across North America reached its lowest level and the species' range was restricted to a fraction of its historical distribution (Hagmeier 1956). In the Eastern and Midwestern United States, martens were found only in limited areas of Maine, New York, and Minnesota (Mech and Rogers 1977).

Harvest records of the late 1800s indicated marten populations were present in localized areas of Minnesota, including Koochiching and Beltrami Counties in the north-central portion of the state. The last marten in Beltrami County was recorded in 1918 (Schorger 1942) and the last marten trapped in northwestern Minnesota was in 1920 from the Northwest Angle. A small population remained in northeastern Minnesota. Protection from trapping in 1933 in conjunction with suspected migration of martens from Ontario resulted in a gradual population increase in northeastern Minnesota during the 1950s and 1960s (Mech and Rogers 1977).

HISTORY OF AMERICAN MARTENS IN WISCONSIN AND MICHIGAN
Pre-reintroduction Status

Protection of martens was too late to prevent extirpation in Wisconsin and Michigan. In Wisconsin, martens once were found at least as far south as Brown, Jackson, Juneau, La Crosse, and St. Croix Counties, following riparian habitats along major rivers. Although the trapping season in Wisconsin was closed in 1921, the last confirmed report of a marten was in 1925 in Douglas County (Jackson 1961). Once found as far south in Michigan as Allegan County, the last confirmed marten sighting in the Lower Peninsula was in 1911

near Lewiston in Montmorency County (Wood and Dice 1924). The more remote Upper Peninsula provided slightly better refuge for the species, where the last confirmed sighting was 1939 in the Huron Mountains in Marquette County (Manville 1948).

Although the value of marten pelts had been lower than that of other furbearer species, the species had been recognized as a "unique and desirable component of wilderness forest ecosystems" (Berg 1982: 165). The reintroduction of martens was expected to fill a "niche in nature" vacated with the species' extirpation (MDNR unpublished). By the 1950s, the amount of continuous forested habitat in the Upper Peninsula was deemed suitable for the survival of marten populations and discussions were initiated on restoring this animal (MDNR unpublished).

Reintroduction and Translocation of Martens in Wisconsin and Michigan
Wisconsin

The reintroduction of martens in Wisconsin began in 1953 with the release of five individuals from near Kalispell, Montana, to Stockton Island, Apostle Islands National Lakeshore, Ashland County (Jordahl 1954; Kohn and Eckstein 1987; Table 3, Fig. 7). No further stocking was undertaken in this area (Kohn and Eckstein 1987).

A large-scale reintroduction in Wisconsin was initiated on January 28, 1975, with the release of eight martens (three females and five males) from the Crown Chapleau Game Preserve (CCGP) to the NFMCA (Davis 1983; Table 4, Fig. 7). On February 27, 1975, 11 martens (two females and nine males) from the CCGP were released on the NNF. Seven martens (one female and six males) from the CCGP were released on the NNF on April 3, 1975. On October 20, 1975, an additional seven martens (one female and six males) from the CCGP

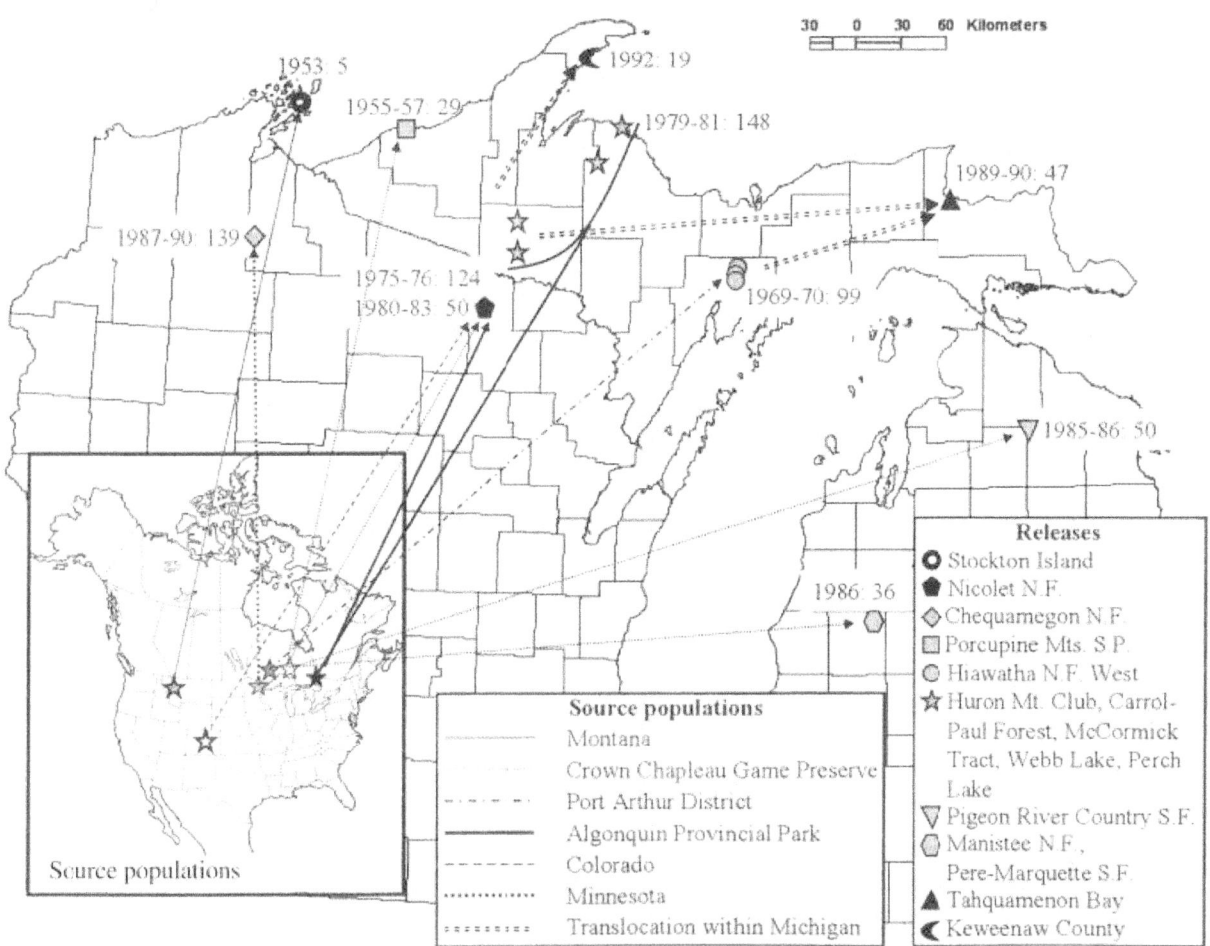

Figure 7.—Release and source locations of reintroductions and translocations of American martens in Michigan and Wisconsin.

were released in the NNF. From December 1975 to April 1976, 91 individuals (20 females and 71 males) trapped in Algonquin Provincial Park (APP), a 7,571-km² park in central Ontario between Georgian Bay and the Ottawa River (Churchill et al. 1981), were part of six releases: 22 martens (five females and 17 males) on December 16, 1975; three males on January 16, 1976; one female and eight males on February 12, 1976; six females and 15 males on March 14, 1976; five females and 14 males on March 25, 1976; and; three females and 14 males on April 2, 1976 (Davis 1983; Table 4, Fig. 7).

A trade was subsequently negotiated to acquire martens from Colorado in exchange for Wisconsin river otters (*Lutra canadensis*, Berg 1982). Between December 1980 and March 1981, 10 females and nine males trapped near Berthoud Pass, Guanella Pass, or Loveland Pass, Colorado, were released on the NNF (J. George,

Colorado Division of Wildlife, pers. commun.). During March of 1981, nine females and nine males from APP were released on the NNF (Wis. Dep. Nat. Resour. 1986). During the winter of 1981 and 1982, two males and two females trapped in Colorado were relocated to the NNF. A final release was made in 1982-83 with nine individuals from Colorado (three females, four males, and two unknown sex). One male from the final release escaped in Minocqua, Wisconsin, on March 14, 1983, while being held at the Northwoods Wildlife Center. One of the unknown individuals died during shipment from Colorado (Wis. Dep. Nat. Resour. 1986). Between 1975 and 1983, 172 martens (51 females, 120 males, and one unknown) were stocked on the FCMA (Table 4, Fig. 7), including seven females and 26 males from the CCGP, 29 females and 80 males from APP, and 15 females, 14 males, and one unknown from Colorado (Wis. Dep. Nat. Resour. 1986).

Table 4.—Demographic data of reintroduction of martens on Nicolet National Forest, Wisconsin

Release location	Date	N (females)	Source population
Nicolet National Forest, Fisher Management Unit, Forest Co.	1/28/1975	8 (3)	Crown Chapleau Game Preserve, Ontario, Canada
	2/27/1975	11 (2)	Crown Chapleau Game Preserve, Ontario, Canada
	4/3/1975	7 (1)	Crown Chapleau Game Preserve, Ontario, Canada
	10/20/1975	7 (1)	Crown Chapleau Game Preserve, Ontario, Canada
	12/16/1975	22 (5)	Algonquin Provincial Park, Ontario, Canada
	1/16/1976	3 (0)	Algonquin Provincial Park, Ontario, Canada
	2/12/1976	9 (1)	Algonquin Provincial Park, Ontario, Canada
	3/14/1976	21 (6)	Algonquin Provincial Park, Ontario, Canada
	3/25/1976	19 (5)	Algonquin Provincial Park, Ontario, Canada
	4/2/1976	17 (3)	Algonquin Provincial Park, Ontario, Canada
	12/80-3/81	19 (10)	Berthoud, Guanella, or Loveland Pass, Colorado
	3/81	18 (9)	Algonquin Provincial Park , Ontario, Canada
	12/81-1/82	4 (2)	Berthoud, Guanella, or Loveland Pass, Colorado
	8/82-3/83	7 (3, 1 Unknown)[a]	Berthoud, Guanella, or Loveland Pass, Colorado
Total:	1975-1983	172 (51)	

[a] Nine martens were trapped, but one male escaped and one marten of unknown sex died prior to release.

Table 5.—Demographic data of reintroductions of martens on Chequamegon National Forest, Wisconsin

Release location	Date	N (females)	Source population
Chequamegon National Forest, Fisher Management Unit, Bayfield and Ashland Counties	1987-1990	139 (45)	Minnesota

In 1987, the WDNR made arrangements to obtain martens from Minnesota for release onto the CNF. Seven trappers were contracted by the Minnesota Department of Natural Resources to capture martens for $100 per individual (Kohn 1991). Of 31 martens procured the first year, only four were females. As a result, a decision was made to continue the live-trapping by WDNR employees. In the fall of 1988, 1989, and 1990, 108 martens (41 females and 67 males) were captured north of Grand Marais in northeastern Minnesota. Between 1987 and 1990, 139 martens (45 females and 94 males) were released on the CNF (Kohn 1991; Table 5, Fig. 7).

Michigan

Marten reintroduction efforts in Michigan were initiated in 1955 in the Porcupine Mountains Wilderness State Park (PMWSP), Ontonagon County by the Michigan Department of Conservation (MDOC), (Switzenberg

Table 6.—Demographic data of reintroduction of martens in Porcupine Mountains Wilderness State Park, Michigan

Release location	Date	N (females)	Source population
Porcupine Mountains Wilderness State Park, Ontonagon County, T51N R42W Sec 18	2/24/1955	4 (2)	White River Country, Algoma District, Ontario, Canada (2); local MI fur farm (2), originally from British Columbia, Canada
	3/29/1955	2 (1)	White River Country, Algoma District, Ontario, Canada
	7/21/1955	1 (0)	Crown Chapleau Game Preserve, Ontario, Canada
	4/11/1956	1 (0)	Crown Chapleau Game Preserve, Ontario, Canada
	2/6/1957	4 (2)	Crown Chapleau Game Preserve, Ontario, Canada
	2/14/1957	8 (4)	Crown Chapleau Game Preserve, Ontario, Canada
	2/19/1957	4 (1)	Crown Chapleau Game Preserve, Ontario, Canada
	2/28/1957	4 (0)	Crown Chapleau Game Preserve, Ontario, Canada
	4/12/1957	1 (1)	Crown Chapleau Game Preserve, Ontario, Canada
Total:	1955-1957	29 (11)	

1955; Table 6, Fig. 7). The release area was dominated by mature hemlock (*Tsuga canadensis*) and other conifers interspersed with openings of sapling- and pole-size hardwoods on rough, broken terrain (MDOC unpublished; Harger and Switzenberg 1958). Two martens (one female and one male) captured by tribal trappers in the White River Country, Algoma District, Ontario, (MDOC interoffice commun.) were released on February 24, 1955. Two martens (one female and one male) purchased from a fur farm run by E. Selander in Perkins, Michigan (MDOC unpublished) also were released on February 24, 1955. The fur farm martens originally were from British Columbia and had been held in captivity for approximately 5 years (Mich. Dep. Conserv. 1957). On March 29, 1955, two martens (one female and one male) from White River Country were released in the PMWSP (MDOC unpublished). A third male from White River Country was scheduled to be released on March 29, 1955, but escaped while being transported between Baraga, Michigan, and the reintroduction site (MDOC unpublished). A single male trapped by the Ontario Department of Lands and Forests (ODLF) in Chapleau County was released in the PMWSP on July 21, 1955 (MDOC unpublished). On February 20, 1956, a female marten held at the Cusino Wildlife Research Station, Shingleton, Michigan, escaped prior to release in the PMWSP (MDOC unpublished). A male from Chapleau County was released in the PMWSP on April 11, 1956, approximately 2.5 km east of the previous releases, in virgin hardwood-hemlock habitat (MDOC unpublished).

The small number of martens (three females and six males) obtained from Ontario for release in 1955 and 1956 was disappointing. Alternative employment opportunities, primarily uranium prospecting, made it difficult to interest the Ontario Indian trappers in capturing martens for Michigan's restoration effort (Mich. Dep. Conserv. 1957). It was apparent that the number of martens released and rate of introduction needed to be increased to facilitate successful restocking (Mich. Dep. Conserv. 1958). In the winter of 1957, three MDOC employees, Al Harger from the Houghton Lake Wildlife Experimental Station, Sid Andrews of Newberry, and John Arduin from Newberry were sent to the CCGP to trap the remaining martens for the PMWSP reintroduction (Harger and Switzenberg 1958).

Table 7.—Demographic data of reintroduction of martens in Hiawatha National Forest, West Unit, Michigan

Release location	Date	N (females)	Source population
Whitefish River Valley, Rapid River Dist., Hiawatha National Forest, West Unit, T43N R20W Sec 29; T42N R20W Secs 7 and 19	4/15/1969	4 (1)	
	4/17/1969	16 (3)	
	4/23/1969	9 (3)	
	5/21/1969	8 (3)	
	6/9/1969	7 (2)	
	10/28/1969	16 (5)	
	11/7/1969	11 (8)	
	12/5/1969	20 (10)	
	3/16/1970	8 (2)	
Total:	*1969-1970*	*99 (37)*	Port Arthur District, Ontario, Canada

The 7,381.5-km^2 CCGP, which has been closed to trapping since 1925, provided refuge for a remnant marten population during range-wide declines in the early 20th century (Harger and Switzenberg 1958). Large areas of coniferous forest, including jack pine (*Pinus banksiana*), black spruce (*Picea mariana*), and balsam fir (*Abies balsamea*), on the CCGP were interspersed with ridges of deciduous forest, including aspen (*Populus* spp.) and white birch (*Betula papyrifera*) (Ludwig 1986).

The three MDOC trappers were located at Camp 6 owned by Newaygo Timber Co., Ltd., a subsidiary of Consolidated Waterpower and Paper Co. of Wisconsin. Camp 6 was located approximately 40 km east of Mosher and 354 km north of Sault Ste. Marie. Assisted by ODLF personnel, the trappers captured 21 martens during February 1957 (Harger and Switzenberg 1958). One animal escaped during transport from the trap-line to Camp 6, one escaped through the back of the trap, and one died during transport to Cusino Wildlife Rearch Station from Sault Ste. Marie (Harger and Switzenberg 1958). Three additional martens were obtained from a fisher-trapping project in Ontario. In all, 21 (eight females and 13 males) were shipped to Michigan (Harger and Switzenberg 1958; Table 6, Fig. 7). On February 6, 1957, two females and two males were released in the PMWSP (MDOC unpublished). Further releases were: four females and four males on February 14, 1957; one

female and three males on February 19, 1957, and four males on February 28, 1957. A pregnant female that had been held at Cusino Wildlife Research Station was released on April 12, 1957 (MDOC unpublished). Some of the martens obtained from Ontario were traded for other species, e.g., sharp-tailed grouse (*Tympanuchus phasianellus*) and wild turkey (*Meleagris gallopavo*) (MDOC interoffice commun.).

A second marten reintroduction in Michigan was initiated in 1969 following assessment of suitable habitat in portions of the HNF. In cooperation with the Forest Service, the MDNR negotiated with Ontario District personnel for the purchase of martens directly from licensed trappers in the former Port Arthur District of Ontario (Mich. Dep. Nat. Resour. 1970). The contact for securing these martens was T. Galarneau, of Nipigon, Ontario and it might be inferred that the animals were captured along his trap-line 40 km north of Nipigon (MDNR interoffice commun.). Thirty-seven females and 62 males were obtained for $37.50 each. Groups of four to 20 animals were flown into Marquette, Michigan from Port Arthur, Ontario, and most were released upon arrival (Mich. Dep. Nat. Resour. 1970). The three release locations were in the Whitefish River Valley, Rapid River District, HNF West Unit (Forest Service interoffice commun.; Table 7, Fig. 7). There were nine releases: one female and three males on April 15, 1969; three

Table 8.—Demographic data of reintroduction of martens into Marquette, Baraga, and Iron Counties, Michigan

Release location	Date	N (females)	Source population
1. Huron Mountain Club, Marquette Co.	1979	38 (8) [a]	
2. Huron Mountain Club, Marquette Co.; Carrol-Paul Forest, Marquette Co.	1980	40 (23)	
3. McCormick Experimental Forest, Ottawa National Forest	1980	22 (13)	
4. Webb Lake, Iron County, Iron River Township, Section 9	1981	10 (6)	
5. Perch Lake area, Iron County, Ottawa National Forest	1981	38 (21)	
Total:	*1979-1981*	*148 (71)*	Algonquin Provincial Park, Ontario, Canada

[a] Thirty-nine martens were trapped, but one male died prior to release.

females and 13 males on April 17, 1969; three females and six males on April 23, 1969; three females and five males on May 21, 1969; two females and five males on June 9, 1969; five females and 11 males on October 28, 1969; eight females and three males on November 7, 1969; 10 females and 10 males on December 5, 1969, and two females and six males on March 16, 1970 (Schupbach 1977). Dry-land trap sets were banned from the 12 townships surrounding the release sites for 5 years beginning on August 1, 1969 to protect the newly released martens from incidental trapping (Mich. Dep. Nat. Resour. 1970).

In 1979, the MDNR contracted trapping and release of a third marten reintroduction event to Michigan Technological University at Houghton (Ontario Ministry of Natural Resources, OMNR, interoffice commun.). The goal was a release of 150 martens. Under the supervision of Dr. Norman Sloan, eight females and 31 males were live-trapped in APP, (OMNR interoffice commun.; Churchill et al. 1981). One male died during shipment to Michigan but the remaining 38 animals were released on the Huron Mountain Club near Lake Superior in northern Marquette County (Churchill et al. 1981; Table 8, Fig. 7). The Huron Mountain Club was privately owned with restricted access, thus offering protection from trapping to released animals (Churchill et al. 1981).

In July 1980, Ecological Research Services, a consulting firm based in Iron River, Michigan, continued the marten relocation efforts supported by the U.S. Endangered Species Program, the MDNR, and the OMNR. Forty martens (23 females and 17 males) from APP were released on the Huron Mountain Club and the adjacent Carrol-Paul Forest in 1980 and 1981 (Churchill et al. 1981; Table 8, Fig. 7). During December 1980, 22 martens (13 females and nine males) from APP were released on the Cyrus H. McCormick Experimental Forest Tract, a 70-km^2 primitive area in Marquette and Baraga Counties (Churchill et al. 1981; Table 8, Fig. 7). The McCormick Tract, a satellite of the ONF closed to motorized vehicle use, consisted of mature mixed hardwoods-conifer, including hemlock, yellow birch (*Betula lutea*), balsam fir, and white pine (*Pinus strobus*) as well as cedar swamps, open areas, and stands of birch (*Betula* spp.) and aspen. The release site was approximately 16 km south of the primary release locations in the Huron Mountains, and was chosen to encourage migration between the two populations (Churchill et al. 1981).

Additional release sites were in the Iron River District of the ONF during the spring of 1981. The general area of release was chosen because of its close proximity to the reintroduced marten population on NFMU-FMCA. A goal of the Iron River releases was to form a link between

Table 9.—Demographic data of reintroductions of martens into Lower Peninsula of Michigan

Release location	Date	N (females)	Source population
Pigeon River Country State Forest, Cheboygan County T33N R1W, Otsego County T31N R1W	11/7/1985	10 (2)	
	11/13/1985	10 (3)	
	11/21/1985	10 (8)	
	11/27/1985	12 (7)	
	12/6/1985	6 (4)	
	3/19/1986	1 (0)	
Total:	*1985-1986*	*49 (24)*	Crown Chapleau Game Preserve, Ontario, Canada
Manistee National Forest	3/5/1986	15 (9)	
Pere-Marquette State Forest	3/12/1986	15 (7)	
Manistee National Forest	3/18/1986	6 (0)	
Total:	*1986*	*36 (16)*	Crown Chapleau Game Preserve, Ontario, Canada

the restricted gene pools of the two reintroductions through migration (Churchill et al. 1981). Ten martens (six females and four males) from APP were released near Webb Lake, approximately 6.5 km northwest of Iron River (Table 8, Fig. 7). This was considered to be a high-density release (3.8 martens/km^2; Churchill et al. 1981). Thirty-eight additional animals (21 females and 17 males) from APP were released north of Webb Lake in 28 sections; this was considered to be a low-density release (approximately 0.6 martens/km^2; Churchill et al. 1981; Table 8, Fig. 7). The low-density releases were about 1 km apart along ONF forest roads (FR) 137, 144-145, and 146. Releases were also made along FR 347 toward Blockhouse Campground, FR 144-145 on the south side of Perch Lake, and along the north side of Perch Lake near the campground. With this final release, 148 martens (71 females and 77 males) had been reintroduced in the west-central Upper Peninsula between 1979 and 1981 (Churchill et al. 1981).

In 1984, the MDNR requested permission from the OMNR to live-trap martens in APP for a series of reintroductions in the northern Lower Peninsula. The restoration effort was planned to occur over 2 to 3 years and entail five to six releases spaced roughly 32 to 64 km apart. Each release was to include about 40 martens for

a total of 220 to 240 animals. The goal was to maintain genetic diversity through natural dispersal among sites. Ten to 15 fishers were expected to be trapped incidentally during the process and would be released to begin the restoration of the fisher to its former range in the northern Lower Peninsula. The OMNR declined permission to trap in APP, in part due to criticism over the removal of wildlife from APP for the Michigan Moose Reintroduction Project. In 1985, the OMNR allowed live-trapping of up to 100 martens in the CCGP (Ludwig 1986).

Ecological Research Services was contracted by the MDNR to undertake the trapping effort in Ontario. The releases were cooperative efforts between the MDNR and the Forest Service. Live-trapping in the CCGP began in late October, 1985. On November 6, 1985, 10 martens (two females and eight males) were shipped to Michigan for release on the Pigeon River Country State Forest (Table 9, Fig. 7). The release area was predominantly forested, consisting of aspen, red pine (*Pinus resinosa*), jack pine, white pine, northern hardwoods, and northern white-cedar (*Thuja occidentalis*)-mixed swamp conifer. The Pigeon River Country State Forest was chosen as a reintroduction site because it included "preferred" marten habitat and was a large tract of public land (Earle

1996). The wide range of habitat types also provided an opportunity to better understand habitat preference and avoidance in land-cover types not found in the source location.

The 10 animals transported in the first group were released on November 7 in Cheboygan County along Fisherman Road., east on Webb Road, and north on Osmun Road. Ten additional martens (three females and seven males) were transported to Michigan on November 12, 1985, and released in Otsego County on November 13 along Tin Bridge Shanty Road, north on House's Lost Cabin Road (Ludwig 1985). On November 21, ten animals (eight females and two males) shipped from Ontario the previous day were released in the Cheboygan and Otsego Counties along Fisherman Road, east on Webb Road, north on Osmun Road, and along Tin Shanty Bridge Road (Ludwig 1985). Twelve martens (seven females and five males) shipped on November 26, 1985, were released the following day in Cheboygan and Otsego Counties along Osmun Road, Webb-Clark, and House's Lost Cabin Road (Ludwig 1985). A final group of six martens (four females and two males) was transported from Ontario on December 5, 1985, and released in Otsego County on December 6 along Hardwood Lake Road, north on Osmun Road to Hemlock Lake (Ludwig 1985).

The reintroduction of martens into the northern Lower Peninsula continued in March 1986. On March 4, nine females and six males were transported by Ecological Research Services from the CCGP and released the following day on the Manistee National Forest (MNF) in Lake and Wexford Counties (For. Serv.-MDNR intraoffice commun.; Table 9, Fig. 7). Seven females and eight males were released on March 12 on the Pere-Marquette State Forest in Lake County (For. Serv.-MDNR intraoffice commun.). The MNF and the Pere-Marquette State Forest were chosen as release sites due to the availability of acceptable marten habitat and the proximity of the two sites meeting qualifications within the Opportunity Area Analysis Plan (Earle 1996). On March 17, six males, three of which were fitted with radio collars, were captured in the CCGP and released the following day on the MNF (For. Serv.-MDNR intraoffice commun.). A juvenile male was transported from the

CCGP on March 18, and was released on the Pigeon River Country State Forest on March 19 (Earle 1996).

The MDNR sought to continue the reintroduction through the winter of 1986-87 by releasing an additional 200 martens into the northern Lower Peninsula. Public sentiment in Ontario had sparked a government review of activities in provincial parks and Crown game preserves, including hunting, trapping, or other removals of animals. The OMNR was concerned that removing 200 martens from any one area of the province could have a negative affect on the remaining population in Ontario. In addition, it was doubtful that the number of beaver carcasses needed for bait could be obtained in time. In the event that live-trapping was allowed and able to proceed given access to needed resources, Ontario trappers would have to be included in the effort (Ecological Research Services-MDNR intraoffice commun.). Ecological Research Services reported that live-trapping in 1985 and 1986 resulted in controversy with the Chapleau local trappers' council. The council believed that Ontario trappers should have been given the opportunity to place a bid on the marten relocation project. The OMNR had initially held a public position that local trappers were not qualified for the project, particularly with respect to handling and anesthesia techniques. The trappers' council and the OMNR finally reached an understanding: local trappers could participate in future release efforts so long as they received proper training (Ecological Research Services-MDNR intraoffice commun.).

There were no additional translocations of martens into the northern Lower Peninsula as a result of the issues mentioned above. Eighty-five martens (40 females and 45 males) had been reintroduced in the Lower Peninsula in 1985 and 1986, including 49 animals (24 females and 25 males) on the Pigeon River Country State Forest, and thirty-six martens (16 females and 20 males) on the MNF and Pere-Marquette State Forest (Ludwig 1986). No additional furbearer species, e.g., fishers or wolverines, were released in the Lower Peninsula.

Translocations were conducted to assist in the dispersal of the marten across its former range in the Upper Peninsula. In the fall of 1989, 20 martens were moved

Table 10.—Demographic data of translocations of martens in Michigan

Release location	Date	N (females)	Source population
1. Tahquamenon Bay, Hiawatha National Forest, East Unit	1989	20	Hiawatha National Forest, West Unit, MI
2. Tahquamenon Bay, Hiawatha National Forest, East Unit	1989-1990	27	Iron County, MI
3. Keweenaw County	1992	19 (5)	Houghton County, MI

by the Forest Service from the West Unit of the HNF to the Tahquamenon Bay area in the HNF East Unit (Table 10, Fig. 7). During the winter of 1989 and 1990, 27 individuals were relocated from Iron County to the Tahquamenon Bay area by the MDNR (Table 10, Fig. 7). In 1992, 19 martens (5 females and 14 males) were moved from southern Houghton County to southeastern Keweenaw County (MDNR unpublished; Table 10, Fig. 7). This last translocation was in conjunction with fisher translocations already in progress.

STATUS OF MARTENS IN WISCONSIN AND MICHIGAN

The marten is the only endangered mammal in Wisconsin. Migration between the NNF population and populations in the Upper Peninsula has been documented (Churchill 1982). It may be that individuals also migrate between the CNF population and populations in Michigan due to the proximity and dispersion of harvested martens in the Upper Peninsula. It is unclear why the species has struggled to expand its range and increase in numbers in Wisconsin while recovering to numbers that allow for harvest only kilometers away in Michigan.

In 1978, the marten was listed as a "state threatened species" in Michigan (Earle et al. 2001). An increase in the number of incidentally trapped martens and field sign resulted in pressure from fur taker organizations to open a trapping season. Martens were removed from Michigan's threatened species list in March 1999. In 2000, a limited trapping season was opened in the Upper Peninsula for the first time since 1924 (Frawley 2002), resulting in harvest of 90 martens (M. Cosgrove,

MDNR, pers. commun.). Since 2000, legal harvests generally have increased; in 2004, 192 martens were trapped. The season bag limit is one per person. Trapping for martens is prohibited in the Lower Peninsula.

REINTRODUCTION THEORY: FISHER AND MARTEN CASE HISTORIES

The goal of any reintroduction is establishment of a self-sustaining population, which is a dynamic process (Sarrazin and Barbault 1996). Surrogate measures of success are frequently used. Because most translocated species are harvested, one goal is to restore abundance to a level that can sustain harvest (Griffith et al. 1989; Slough 1994). Success can be defined subjectively by numerically abundant and widely distributed individuals of a reintroduced population. Obtaining high genetic diversity is another important goal of reintroduction programs (e.g., Allendorf and Leary 1986; Leberg 1990; Frankham 1995).

Strategies for successful population reintroduction include use of large numbers of founding individuals, high genetic variation among founding individuals, and the occurrence of refugia (Griffith et al. 1989). Following release, a high rate of population increase and low effect of competition will increase probability of successful reintroduction. Fisher and marten populations in Michigan and Wisconsin allow us to examine the effects of multiple reintroductions into areas from which both species were extirpated. The data in this report can be used in conjunction with genetics and ecological data to test predictions related to founder events and assist in the design, application, and assessment of future reintroductions.

Assessment of Reintroductions of Fishers

In Wisconsin, the estimated average rate of fisher population expansion was about 3 km per year (Gilbert 2000). The population initiated on the CNF seemed to have expanded at a greater rate than the population originating on the NNF (Petersen et al. 1977). Although the numbers released at each area were identical, the period during which those releases occurred and the sex ratios might have resulted in differences in overall population expansion. All fishers were stocked on the CNF over an 11-month period with a balanced sex ratio (30 females and 30 males). Fishers were stocked sporadically in the NNF over 7 years with a male-biased sex ratio (36 males and 24 females). Fishers from the NNF reintroduction likely spread into the Upper Peninsula and contributed to expansion north and east; this was undocumented by the WDNR.

The MDNR began a formal survey of accidentally trapped or road killed fishers (Cooley et al. 1982) with the examination of eight carcasses during the winter of 1981. The fishers were collected in Gogebic, Ontonagon, Houghton, Baraga, Iron, and Marquette Counties in the western Upper Peninsula (Cooley et al. 1982). The number of fishers accidentally killed increased in the following years, peaking at 50 in both 1987 and 1988 (Cooley et al. 1986, 1987, 1988).

In 1989, fishers were considered abundant in much of the western Upper Peninsula (Cooley et al. 1990). As a result, limited trapping was allowed in Baraga, Gogebic, Houghton, Iron, Marquette, and Ontonagon Counties on 12,276.5 km^2 in the western Upper Peninsula known as Fisher Management Unit A (Sodders 1999; Cooley et al. 2001). The original harvest season was designed to be conservative and was limited to 11 days in December with a bag limit of one fisher per trapper. Registration of all captured fishers was mandatory. In 1993, the bag limit was increased to three per trapper. In 1994, fisher trapping was expanded to include Fisher Management Unit B (west-central Upper Peninsula), which included Alger, Delta, Dickinson, Houghton, Keweenaw, Marquette, and Menominee Counties. This increased the trapping area to 26,231.4 km^2 (Sodders 1999). The season bag limit in Unit B was one fisher

per trapper. The remaining 15,920.7 km^2 of the eastern Upper Peninsula (except Drummond Island) was opened to fisher trapping in 1996 and added to Unit B (Cooley et al. 2001). The bag limit remained at one fisher per trapper in Unit B (Cooley et al. 2001). Current regulations continue to allow three fishers per trapper, one of which can be taken in Unit B (Mich. Dep. Nat. Resour. 2005).

Assessment of Reintroductions of Martens
Wisconsin

A single marten was observed on Stockton Island, Wisconsin, during the winter of 1971-72, nearly 20 years following reintroduction (Schupbach 1977; Davis 1978). There were no further reports made and the reintroduction was considered a failure (Kohn and Eckstein 1987).

Davis (1978) conducted a study in 1975-76 to evaluate the reintroduction of martens on the NNF. Several martens were radio-tracked and in combination with winter track counts and other observations it was determined that the species populated the area surrounding the releases immediately following the effort. Relatively few females had been included in the release (27 females of a total of 124) and no reproduction had been reported (Davis 1978, 1983). Without further releases, the final outcome of the reintroduction was uncertain (Davis 1978).

By 1986, the marten population on the NNF was estimated to be 150 to 200 individuals. The population was projected to reach 300 individuals by 1990 (Wisc. Dep. Nat. Resour. 1986), but was estimated at 221 +/- 61 in 2006 (Woodford et al. 2006). The current marten population remains concentrated within 20 km of the original release sites (unpublished).

Martens have remained in and around the area of the reintroduction on the CNF and breeding has occurred (unpublished). On the CNF, Forest Service and GLIFWC scientists are studying habitat use and selection as well as population size and range of martens. Currently, the marten population on the CNF is thought to be about 40 individuals (unpublished).

Michigan

Martens are unlikely prolific colonizers, and often are slow to expand their range.[2] American martens have a strong homing instinct (Harger and Switzenberg 1958). On July 28, 1955, the male fur farm animal released in the PMWSP 5 months earlier was found dead on Route 2 in Masonville, 225 km from the release site, and about 10 km from the fur farm (Harger and Switzenberg 1958). Ludwig (1986) found evidence of homing instincts in males that were captured and released in APP during the live-trapping program in 1985 and 1986. For example, a male (M-138) captured in APP on March 15, 1986 was released 55 km from the trap site. The following day, M-138 was captured in the same initial trap (Ludwig 1986). The tendency toward a strong homing instinct could be problematic for marten reintroduction efforts as individuals may not remain in the release area (MDOC interoffice commun.).

At the time of the first reintroduction in Michigan, MDOC personnel were aware of the strong homing instinct of martens and believed that releasing a sufficient number of animals in a given area should result in several martens establishing territories. It also was believed that a successful reintroduction would be linked to females. One female assumed to be pregnant was held at the Cusino Wildlife Experiment Station for release in April, near the time when she would give birth. It was believed that the resulting maternal instinct would overcome the homing instinct and that the female with her kits would remain near the release area (Harger and Switzenberg 1958). The result of the female's pregnancy was undetermined (MDOC interoffice commun.).

In the years immediately following the marten releases in the PMWSP, many sightings of martens were reported, though few were considered valid. The MDOC ran systematic survival checks in the area surrounding the release site. Routes were traveled via foot, truck, and tracked vehicle in search of marten tracks. Survival checks in 1957 and 1958 resulted in documentation of few fresh tracks (Mich. Dep. Conserv. 1958, 1960; Schupbach

1977). Surveys conducted in December through January 1958-59 and February through March of 1960 included attempts to live-trap existing martens. No martens were trapped during either period (Switzenberg and Laycock 1961). A minimum of two fresh marten tracks was recorded during the 1958-59 checks. No tracks were observed during the 1960 effort or during an additional survey undertaken in 1965. The lack of marten sightings in the area surrounding the release site led to the conclusion that the reintroduction attempt had failed (Mich. Dep. Conserv. 1966). Winter track surveys and harvest records are currently being used to gauge population status and distribution (Earle 2002; Frawley 2002). Both methods indicate that martens inhabit areas near the original release site (e.g., Fig. 8). Animals in these areas may be products of the original reintroduction or dispersal from later relocation efforts from Michigan or Wisconsin.

Records of sightings of live martens as well as tracks and carcasses were compiled by the MDNR following the reintroduction of 1969 and 1970 in the Whitefish River Valley. By 1977, 59 records documented a wide dispersal of martens from their release locations on the HNF, West Unit. Martens were sighted along the Lake Superior shore north of the HNF, along the Lake Michigan shore to the south, Ontonagon County to the northwest, and Luce and Mackinac Counties to the east (Fig. 9). The average reported distance from the reintroduction sites was 40 km, though martens were observed as far away as 180 km (Schupbach 1977). During January and February of 1976 and 1977, Schupbach (1977) surveyed an area of 673 km^2 surrounding the Delta County reintroduction site for signs of martens, but no tracks were discovered. Local trappers and residents also reported few sightings. Schupbach (1977) estimated that fewer than 50 martens inhabited the survey area. Illegal dry-set trapping, incidental takes in wet-set traps, and random shooting of martens were cited as inhibiting the establishment of a stable population in the area surrounding the 1969-70 reintroduction. The scattered nature of reports and lack of juveniles (untagged individuals) away from this area suggested that it was highly unlikely that a breeding nucleus could exist elsewhere in the Upper Peninsula (Schupbach 1977). Current MDNR winter track-count surveys and harvest records indicate a limited presence of

---

[2]Bostick, D. (Huron-Manistee National Forests). 2002-2003 American marten winter track count monitoring project. Final report (unpublished).

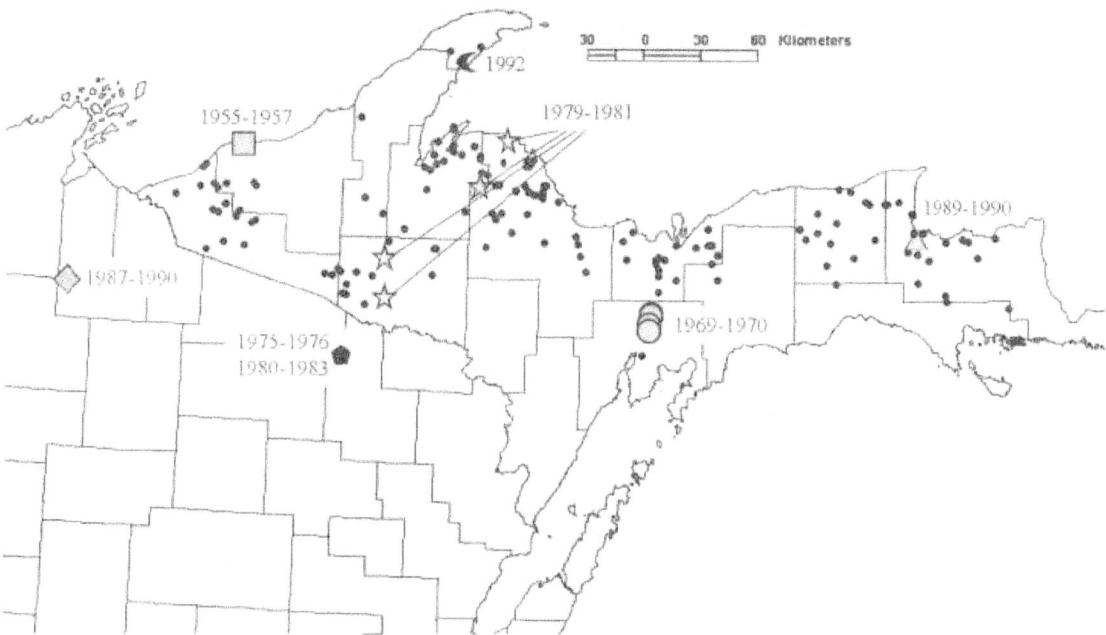

Figure 8.—Distribution of reported marten harvests in the Upper Peninsula of Michigan from 2000 to 2004 (reintroduction and translocation sites and dates are added for reference).

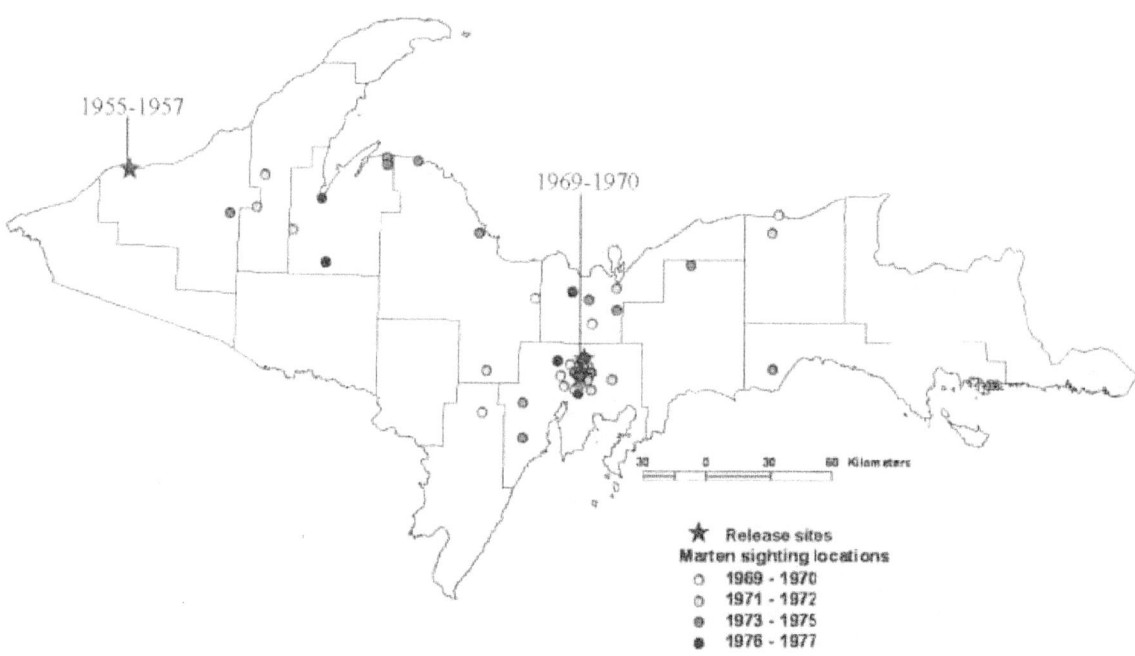

Figure 9.—Reports of marten sightings in the Upper Peninsula of Michigan from April 1969 to October 1977; adapted from Schupbach (1977).

martens in this area of the HNF. A number of individuals have been detected 20 to 40 km to the north, suggesting that martens reintroduced in 1969 and 1970 may have dispersed and established territories toward Lake Superior (Figs. 8-9). If this was the case, the reintroduction was successful in founding a persisting population.

Martens reported in Luce and Mackinac Counties from 1969 to 1977, assuming the sightings were valid, could only have been products of the 1969-70 reintroduction due to the distance and direction from all previous release locations. Individuals reported in Ontonagon and Baraga Counties may have resulted from the 1955-57 releases in the PMWSP or the 1969-70 releases in the Whitefish River Valley.

During the winter of 1981-82, Ecological Research Services enacted a live-trapping program around the reintroduction sites of 1979, 1980, and 1981 to assess the survival and dispersal of released martens. Five martens that had been part of the original release were trapped on the Huron Mountain Club near their initial release site; they were deemed to be in good to excellent condition (Churchill et al. 1982). Seven martens were captured in Iron County during the live-trapping effort. Five of the seven animals, including an unmarked juvenile, were trapped near the Perch Lake and Winslow Lake areas where most of the martens had been released. One female was captured approximately 24 km from her original release site. One male was captured nearly 23 km from his NNF release site (Churchill et al. 1982).

The relocations into the northern Lower Peninsula of Michigan in 1985 and 1986 were not intended as stand-alone events. The release sites in the Pigeon River Country State Forest and the MNF-Pere-Marquette State Forest were separated by more than 160 km, resulting in potential geographic isolation of the restocked populations. Some limited exchange between the two populations has been suggested, but the area between the two marten populations in the northern Lower Peninsula is fragmented by agricultural land, highways, and urban areas. Martens are considered habitat specialists and are not known for rapid range expansion or colonization, particularly when preferred habitat is limited.[2] Fragmentation of habitat is negatively correlated with marten numbers (e.g., Hargis and Bissonnette 1997).

CONSIDERATIONS FOR FUTURE MARTEN RELEASES

Strategies for successful population reintroduction include using a large number of founding individuals, high genetic variation among founding individuals,

low effect of competition at the release site, and the occurrence of refugia (Griffith et al. 1989). Releases consisting of equal or female-biased sex ratios have been deemed more likely to promote a viable population. Each reintroduction effort into Wisconsin and Michigan was characterized by different numbers, sex ratios and sources of martens released, release techniques, and time spans over which the releases occurred. These data along with knowledge of the current status of marten populations can provide valuable insights for the future management of these species.

A large number of founding individuals is expected to increase probability of successful reintroduction. No relationship between number of founders and reintroduction success was apparent in Wisconsin or Michigan. The reintroduction events on the CNF and NNF involved a large number of founders (139 and 174 martens, respectively), but the species remains State Endangered. Conversely, the number of reintroduced founders in Michigan ranged from 29 to 148, and martens are harvested annually.

The time span during which reintroductions occur might affect the probability of population establishment following reintroduction. The 1955-57 PMWSP release, the 1969-70 Whitefish River Valley reintroduction, and the 1975-83 NNF reintroduction consisted of small releases often of 10 or fewer individuals over 2 or more years (Tables 4, 6, 7). The total number of martens released is deceptive: the number released at one time or even during a single season might be too low to expect the establishment of a viable breeding population, particularly given high emigration rates due to strong homing instinct.

High genetic diversity among founding individuals might be achieved by using individuals from multiple sources. Six source populations were used to reintroduce martens into Michigan and Wisconsin. With the exception of Colorado and Montana, all source populations were historically part of a contiguous range of martens across Ontario and into the Upper Midwest. Human disturbance, including habitat fragmentation and exploitation, created a number of smaller disjunct refugia where martens remained into the 20th century.

Individuals in these refugia may be adapted to local environmental conditions. Local adaptation, even if subtle, may result in an unfavorable response of individuals to relocation. Prey should drive habitat preference and selection but relocated martens may disperse in search of forest types similar to their source area.

Competition or predation might reduce the probability of successful reintroduction even when refugia are available. Marten reintroductions were attempted nearly 15 years following the reintroduction of fishers on the NNF and 30 years after fisher reintroduction on the CNF. Although martens were released in areas closed to trapping, thereby protecting establishing individuals from harvest mortality, interspecific competition with or predation by fishers might have been limiting. In the PMWSP and on the HNF, West Unit, marten reintroductions occurred before the reintroduction of fishers into each area. Conversely, the 1979-81 releases into the west-central Upper Peninsula occurred 20 years following fisher reintroduction. Study of fisher densities in areas coincident with marten populations in Wisconsin and Michigan would provide insight into species interactions.

Davis (1983) suggested that female-biased sex ratios should be used for short-term releases but that a restoration effort spanning several years should consist of a release of equal numbers of males and females. Reintroduction occurring near time of parturition may decrease homing instinct of pregnant females (i.e., long-range dispersal patterns) and increase the probability of establishing local territories due to strong maternal instinct (de Vos and Guenther 1952; Harger and Switzenberg 1958).

The method of release is another consideration in promoting successful reintroduction. Two techniques were used during the 1975-76 marten release on the NNF. Individuals that were "quick-released" were liberated within 24 hours of arrival on site. The quick-release technique was used for most of the reintroductions and translocations in Wisconsin and Michigan (Slough 1994). A second technique involved "gentle-released" animals that were held at relocation sites in pens for about 7 days prior to liberation. Five quick-released males, five quick-released females, four gentle-released males, and six gentle-released females were radio-collared to examine post-release movement patterns. Dispersal from the release site appeared to be limited by the gentle-release technique (Davis 1983), but similar results might have been obtained if release of pregnant females occurred close to parturition, or if food items, such as deer carcasses were placed at the release site (Davis 1983). The quick- and gentle-release techniques were compared for martens released on the Huron Mountain Club in 1979 and 1980 (Churchill et al. 1982). No differences were found between the release techniques in the post-release movements or establishment of territories.

ACKNOWLEDGMENTS

We thank the following individuals who contributed materials for this report: Neil Dawson, Lynn Landriault, Rosemary Hartley, and Jim Rettie (OMNR), Steve Babler (USDA Forest Service), Doug Wagner and Dwayne Etter (MDNR), Bruce Kohn (WDNR, retired), Jim Woodford (WDNR), and Damien Lunning. We thank Kim Scribner (Michigan State University) for his support as the M.S. advisor for B.W.W. We also thank Roger Powell (North Carolina State University), Bob Brander (USDA Forest Service, retired), and Bruce Kohn for their helpful reviews of the manuscript.

LITERATURE CITED

Allen, G.M. 1904. **Check list of the mammals of New England**. Occasional Papers of the Boston Society of Natural History. 7: 1-35.

Allen, J.A. 1876. **The former range of some New England mammals**. American Naturalist. 10: 27-32.

Allendorf, F.W.; Leary, R.F. 1986. **Heterozygosity and fitness in natural populations of animals**. In: Soule, M.E., ed. Conservation biology: the science of scarcity and diversity. Sunderland, MA: Sinauer Associates: 57-76.

Aubry, K.B.; Houston, D.B. 1992. **Distribution and status of the fisher in Washington**. Northwestern Naturalist. 73: 69-79.

Audubon, J.J.; Bachman, J. 1851-1854. **The quadrupeds of North America**. New York: V.G. Audubon.

Baily, V. 1931. **Mammals of New Mexico**. Bur. of Biol. Surv., North Am. Fauna, No. 53. Washington, DC: U. S. Department of. Agriculture.

Baird, S.F. 1859. **Mammals of North America; the descriptions of species based chiefly on the collections in the Museum of the Smithsonian Institution**. Philadephia, PA: J.B. Lippincott & Co.

Bell, R. 1884. **Observations on the geology, mineralogy, zoology, and botany of the Labrador coast, Hudson's Strait, and Bay**. Progress Report of the Geological Survey, Canada 1882-83. 4: 1-62DD.

Benson, D.A. 1959. **The fisher in Nova Scotia**. Journal of Mammalogy. 40: 451.

Berg, W.E. 1982. **Reintroduction of fisher, pine marten, and river otter**. In: Sanderson, G.C., ed. Midwest furbearer management. Wichita, KS: The Wildlife Society, Central Mountains and Plains Section: 158-173.

Bradle, B.J. 1957. **The fisher returns to Wisconsin**. Wisconsin Conservation Bulletin. 22: 9-11.

Brander, R.B.; Books, D.J. 1973. **Return of the fisher**. Natural History. 82: 52-57.

Brayton, A.W. 1882. **Report on the mammals of Ohio**. Report of the Geological Survey of Ohio. 4: 3-185.

Burt, W.H. 1948. **The mammals of Michigan**. 2nd ed. Ann Arbor, MI: University of Michigan Press.

Cahalane, V.H. 1947. **The mammals of North America**. New York: Macmillan.

Churchill, S.J.; Herman, L.A.; Herman, M.F.; Ludwig, J.P. 1981. **Final report on the completion of the Michigan marten reintroduction program**. Iron River, MI: Ecological Research Services.

Churchill, S.J.; Herman, L.A.; Ludwig, J.P. 1982. **A report on the winter 1981-1982 Michigan marten livetrapping program**. Iron River, MI: Ecological Research Services.

Cook, D.B.; Hamilton, W.J., Jr. 1957. **The forest, the fisher, and the porcupine**. Journal of Forestry. 55: 719-722.

Cooley, T.M.; Schmitt, S.M.; Friedrich, P.D. 1982. **Fisher survey—1981-1982**. Rep. No. 2918. Lansing, MI: Michigan Department of Natural Resources, Wildlife Division.

Cooley, T.M.; Schmitt, S.M.; Friedrich, P.D. 1986. **Fisher survey—1984, 1985, 1986**. Rep. No. 3034. Lansing, MI: Michigan Department of Natural Resources, Wildlife Division.

Cooley, T.M.; Schmitt, S.M.; Friedrich, P.D. 1987. **Fisher survey—1985, 1986, 1987**. Rep. No. 3062. Lansing, MI: Michigan Department of Natural Resources, Wildlife Division.

Cooley, T.M.; Schmitt, S.M.; Friedrich, P.D. 1988. **Fisher survey—1987, 1988**. Rep. No. 3081. Lansing, MI: Michigan Department of Natural Resources, Wildlife Division.

Cooley, T.M.; Schmitt, S.M.; Friedrich, P.D; Stuht, J.N. 1990. **Fisher survey—1989**. Rep. No. 3126. Lansing, MI: Michigan Department of Natural Resources, Wildlife Division.

Cooley, T.M.; Schmitt, S.M.; Friedrich, P.D; Stuht, J.N. 1991. **Fisher survey—1990**. Rep. No. 3140. Lansing, MI: Michigan Department of Natural Resources, Wildlife Division.

Cooley, T.M.; Schmitt, S.M.; Friedrich, P.D.; Reis, T.F. 1992. **Fisher survey—1991**. Rep. No. 3172. Lansing, MI: Michigan Department of Natural Resources, Wildlife Division.

Cooley, T.M.; Schmitt, S.M.; Friedrich, P.D.; Reis, T.F. 1993. **Fisher survey—1992**. Rep. No. 3189. Lansing,

MI: Michigan Department of Natural Resources, Wildlife Division.

Cooley, T.M.; Schmitt, S.M.; Friedrich, P.D.; Reis, T.F. 1994. **Fisher survey—1993**. Rep. No. 3215. Lansing, MI: Michigan Department of Natural Resources, Wildlife Division.

Cooley, T.M.; Schmitt, S.M.; Friedrich, P.D.; Reis, T.F. 1995. **Fisher survey-1994**. Rep. No. 3239. Lansing, MI: Michigan Department of Natural Resources, Wildlife Division.

Cooley, T.M.; Schmitt, S.M.; Friedrich, P.D.; Reis, T.F. 1997a. **Fisher survey—1995**. Rep. No. 3258. Lansing, MI: Michigan Department of Natural Resources, Wildlife Division.

Cooley, T.M.; Schmitt, S.M.; Friedrich, P.D.; Reis, T.F. 1997b. **Fisher survey—1996**. Rep. No. 3264. Lansing, MI: Michigan Department of Natural Resources, Wildlife Division.

Cooley, T.M.; Schmitt, S.M.; Friedrich, P.D.; Reis, T.F. 1998. **Fisher survey—1997**. Rep. No. 3286. Lansing, MI: Michigan Department of Natural Resources, Wildlife Division.

Cooley, T.M.; Schmitt, S.M.; Friedrich, P.D.; Reis, T.F. 2001. **Fisher survey—1999**. Rep. No. 3329. Lansing, MI: Michigan Department of Natural Resources, Wildlife Division.

Davis, M.H. 1978. **Reintroduction of the pine marten into the Nicolet National Forest, Forest County, Wisconsin**. Stevens Point, WI: University of Wisconsin. M.S. thesis.

Davis, M.H. 1983. **Post-release movements of introduced marten**. Journal of Wildlife Management. 47: 59-66.

Davis, T. 1997. **'Fishers'.** Wisconsin Trails. January/February: 27-30.

de Vos, A. 1951. **Recent findings in fisher and marten ecology and management**. Transactions of the Sixteenth North American Wildlife Conference. 16: 498-507.

de Vos, A.; Guenther, S.E. 1952. **Preliminary live-trapping studies of martens**. Journal of Wildlife Management. 16: 207-214.

Dhuey, B.; Kohn, B.; Olson, J. 2000. **Fisher harvest 2000**. Madison, WI: Wisconsin Department of Natural Resources.

Earle, R.D. 1978. **The fisher-porcupine relationship in Upper Michigan**. Houghton, MI: Michigan Technological University, Department of Biological Sciences. M.S. thesis.

Earle, R.D. 1996. **Winter habitat preferences of marten**. MDNR job final report. Proj. W-127-R-14, Stud. 127-20. Lansing, MI: Michigan Department of Natural Resources.

Earle, R.D. 2002. **Furbearer winter track count survey of 2001**. Rep. No. 3366. Lansing, MI: Michigan Department of Natural Resources, Wildlife Division.

Earle, R.D.; Mastenbrook, L.H.; Reis, T.F. 2001. **Distribution and abundance of the American marten in northern Michigan**. Rep. No. 3321. Michigan Department of Natural Resources, Wildlife Division.

Emmons, E. 1840. **Report on the quadrupeds of Massachusetts**. In: Dewey, C.; Emmons, E., eds. Reports on the herbaceous plants and on the quadrupeds of Massachusetts. Cambridge, MA: Folsom Wells and Thurston.

Frankham, R. 1995. **Conservation genetics**. Annual Review of Genetics. 29: 305-327.

Frawley, B.J. 2002. **2001 marten harvest survey**. Rep. No. 3369. Lansing, MI: Michigan Department of Natural Resources, Wildlife Division.

Fuller, R.W. 1975. **The 1974 fisher trapping season in Vermont**. [Vermont] Game Annual: 23-30.

Gibilisco, C.J. 1994. **Distributional dynamics of modern *Martes* in North America**. In: Buskirk, S.W.; Harestad, A. S.; Raphael, M. G.; Powell, R. A., eds. Martens, sables, and fishers: biology and conservation. Ithaca, NY: Comstock Publishing Associates: 59-71.

Gilbert, J.H. 2000. **Impacts of reestablished fisher on Wisconsin's bobcat population**. Madison, WI: University of Wisconsin. Ph.D. dissertation.

Griffth, B.; Scott, J.M.; Carpenter, J.W.; Reed, C. 1989. **Translocation as a species conservation tool: status and strategy**. Science. 477-480.

Grinnel, J.; Dixon, J.; Lindsdale, J.M. 1937. **Fur-bearing mammals of California: their natural history, systematic status, and relation to man**. Berkeley, CA: University of California Press.

Hagmeier, E.M. 1956. **Distribution of marten and fisher in North America**. Canadian Field-Naturalist. 70: 101-148.

Harger, E.M.; Switzenberg, D.F. 1958. **Returning the pine marten to Michigan**. Rep. 2199. Lansing, MI: Michigan Department of Conservation, Game Division.

Hargis, C.D.; Bissonnette, J.A.. 1997. **Effects of forest fragmentation on populations of American marten in the Intermountain West**. In: Proulx, G.; Bryant, H.N.; Woodard, P.M., eds. Martes: taxonomy, ecology, techniques and management. Edmonton, AB: Provincial Museum of Alberta: 437-451.

Harris, L.D.; Maser, C.; McKee, A. 1982. **Patterns of old growth harvest and implications for Cascades wildlife**. Transactions of the North American Wildlife Natural Resources Conference. 47: 374-392.

Hine, R.L.; Nicotera, R.F.; Christenson, L.M.; Germain, C.E.; Hale, J.B.; Hettrick, H.D.; Les, B.; Posekany, L.A. 1975. **Endangered animals in Wisconsin**.

Madison, WI: Wisconsin Department of Natural Resources.

Hubert, G.F., Jr. 1982. **History of Midwestern furbearer management and a look to the future**. In: Sanderson, G.C., ed. Midwest furbearer management. Wichita, KS: The Wildlife Society, Central Mountains and Plains Section: 174-191.

Irvine, G.W. 1961. **Progress report on the porcupine problem on the Ottawa National Forest**. Ironwood, MI: U.S. Department of Agriculture, Forest Service, Ottawa National Forest.

Irvine, G.W. 1962. **Fisher restoration project progress report**. Ironwood, MI: U.S. Department of Agriculture, Forest Service, Ottawa National Forest.

Irvine, G.W.; Brander, R.B. 1971. **Progress report on a fisher-porcupine study on the Ottawa National Forest**. Ironwood, MI: U.S. Department of Agriculture, Forest Service, Ottawa National Forest.

Irvine, G.W.; Magnus, L.T.; Bradle, B.J. 1964. **The restocking of fisher in Lake States forests**. Transactions of the North American Wildlife and Resource Conference. 29: 307-315.

Jackson, H.H.T. 1961. **Mammals of Wisconsin**. Madison, WI: University of Wisconsin Press.

Jordahl, C.J. 1954. **Marten are back!** Wisconsin Conservation Bulletin. 19: 26-28.

Kellogg, R. 1937. **Annotated list of West Virginia mammals**. Proceedings of the U.S. Natural Museum. 84: 443-447.

Kennicott, R.I. 1855. **Catalogue of animals observed in Cook County, Illinois**. Transactions of the Illinois State Agricultural Society. 1: 577-595.

Kirk, G.L. 1916. **The mammals of Vermont**. Joint Bulletin of the Vermont Botany and Bird Clubs: 28-34.

Kohn, B.E. 1991. **Minnesota pine martens introduced to Wisconsin**. The Niche. Newsletter of the Wisconsin Bureau of Endangered Resources. 5: 4.

Kohn, B.E.; Eckstein, R.G. 1987. **Status of marten in Wisconsin, 1985**. Res. Rep. 143. Madison, WI: Wisconsin Department of Natural Resources, Bureau of Research.

Krohn, W.B.; Elowe, K.D.; Boone, R.B. 1995. **Relations among fishers, snow, and martens: development and evaluation of two hypotheses**. Forestry Chronicle. 71: 97-105.

Krohn, W.B.; Zielinkski, W.J.; Boone, R.B. 1997. **Relations among fishers, snow, and martens in California: results from small-scale spatial comparisons**. In: Proulx, G.; Bryant, H.N.; Woodard, P.M., eds. Martes: taxonomy, ecology, techniques, and management. Edmonton, Alberta: Provincial Museum of AB: 211-232.

Leberg, P.L. 1990. **Genetic considerations in the design of introduction programs**. Transactions of the North American Wildlife and Natural Resources Conference. 55: 609-619.

Ludwig, J.P. 1985. **Internal progress report on fall 1985 marten trapping project in the Chapleau Provincial Game Preserve**. Boyne City, MI: Ecological Research Services.

Ludwig, J.P. 1986. **A short report on the Michigan marten reintroduction program Lower Peninsula in 1985-86: comparison to trapping success with the Algonquin Park efforts of 1980-81**. Boyne City, MI: Ecological Research Services.

Macleod, C.F. 1950. **The productivity and distribution of fur-bearing species of the coast forest of British Columbia in relation to some environmental factors**. Vancouver, BC: University of British Columbia. M.A. thesis.

Manville, R.H. 1948. **The vertebrate fauna of the Huron Mountains, Michigan**. American Midland Naturalist. 39: 615-640.

Mech, L.D.; Rogers, L.L. 1977. **Status, distribution, and movements of martens in northeastern Minnesota**. Res. Pap. NC-143. St. Paul, MN: U.S. Department of Agriculture, Forest Service, North Central Forest Experiment Station. 7 p.

Michigan Department of Conservation. 1957. **Current status of pine marten releases in Upper Peninsula**. Spec. Rep. 14. Shingleton, MI: Michigan Department of Conservation, Cusino Wildlife Experiment Station.

Michigan Department of Conservation. 1958. **19th biennial report of the Department of Conservation of the State of Michigan, 1957-1958**. Lansing, MI: Michigan Department of Conservation.

Michigan Department of Conservation. 1960. **20th biennial report of the Department of Conservation of the State of Michigan, 1959-1960**. Lansing, MI: Michigan Department of Conservation.

Michigan Department of Conservation. 1966. **23rd biennial report of the Department of Conservation of the State of Michigan, 1965-1966**. Lansing, MI: Michigan Department of Conservation.

Michigan Department of Natural Resources. 1970. **25th biennial report of the Department of Natural Resources of the State of Michigan, 1969-1970**. Lansing, MI: Michigan Department of Natural Resources.

Michigan Department of Natural Resources. 1990. **Fisher management plan**. Lansing, MI: Michigan Department of Natural Resources, Wildlife Division.

Michigan Department of Natural Resources. 2005. **2005 Michigan hunting and trapping guide**. Lansing, MI: Michigan Department of Natural Resources.

Olson, H.F. 1966. **Return of a native**. Wisconsin Conservation Bulletin. 31: 22-23.

Pack, J.C.; Cromer, J.I. 1981. **Reintroduction of fisher in West Virginia**. In: Chapman, J.A.; Pursley, D., eds. Worldwide furbearer conference proceedings, vol. 2: Frostburg, MD: Frostburg State College: 1431-1442.

Petersen, L.R.; Martin, M.A.; Pils, C.M. 1977. **Status of fishers in Wisconsin, 1975**. Res. Rep. 92. Madison, WI: Wisconsin Department of Natural Resources.

Plummer, J.T. 1844. **Scraps in natural history (quadrupeds)**. American Journal of Science. 46: 236-249.

Powell, R.A. 1993. **The fisher: life history, ecology, and behavior**. Minneapolis, MN: University of Minnesota Press.

Raine, R.M. 1983. **Winter habitat use and responses to snow of fisher (*Martes pennanti*) and marten (*Martes americana*) in southeastern Manitoba**. Canadian Journal of Zoology. 61: 25-34.

Rand, A.L. 1944. **The status of the fisher *Martes pennanti* (Erxleben) in Canada**. Canadian Field Naturalist. 58: 85-96.

Richardson, J. 1829. **Fauna boreali-americana; or the zoology of the northern parts of British North America: containing descriptions of the objects of natural history collected on the late northern lands expeditions, under command of Captain Sir John Franklin, R.N. Part first containing the quadrupeds**. London: John Murray.

Rhoads, S.N. 1896. **Contributions to the biology of Tennessee, no. 3**. Proceedings of the Academy of Natural Sciences of Philadelphia. 48: 175-205.

Rhoads, S.N. 1898. **Contributions to a revision of the North American beavers, otters and fishers**. Transactions of the American Philosophical Society. 19: 417-439.

Rhoads, S.N. 1903. **The mammals of Pennsylvania and New Jersey**. Philadelphia, PA: [Publisher name unknown].

Sarrazin, F.; Barbault, R. 1996. **Reintroduction: challenges and lessons for basic ecology**. Trends in Ecology and Evolution. 11: 474-478.

Schoonmaker, W.J. 1938. **The fisher as a foe of the porcupine in New York State**. Journal of Mammalogy. 19: 373-374.

Schorger, A.W. 1942. **Extinct and endangered mammals and birds of the Upper Great Lakes Region**. Transactions of the Wisconsin Academy of Sciences, Arts, and Letters. 34: 23-44.

Schupbach, T.A. 1977. **History, status, and management of the pine marten in the Upper Peninsula of Michigan**. Houghton, MI: Michigan Technological University. M.S. thesis.

Seton, E.T. 1925-1928. **Lives of game animals**. New York: Doubleday Doran.

Skinner, M.P. 1927. **The predatory and fur-bearing animals of Yellowstone National Park**. Roosevelt Wildlife Bulletin. 4: 156-281.

Slough, B.G. 1994. **Translocations of American martens**. In: Buskirk, S. W.; Harestad, A. S.; Raphael, M. G.; Powell, R. A., eds. Martens, sables, and fishers: biology and conservation. Ithaca, NY: Comstock Publishing Associates: 165-178.

Sodders, B. 1999. **'Comeback carnivore'**. Michigan Out-of-Doors. February: 8, 39.

Steck, M. 1988. **A translocation of fisher in the Upper Peninsula of Michigan**. Final Rep. Lansing, MI: Michigan Department of Natural Resources.

Steck, M. 1989. **The 1989 translocation of fisher in the Upper Peninsula of Michigan**. Final Rep. Lansing, MI: Michigan Department of Natural Resources.

Steck, M. 1990. **The 1990 translocation of fisher in the Upper Peninsula of Michigan**. Final Rep. Lansing, MI: Michigan Department of Natural Resources.

Switzenberg, D.F. 1955. **Report on first release of Canadian pine martens (*Martes americana*) in Upper Peninsula**. Rep. 2040. Lansing, MI: Michigan Department of Conservation, Game Division.

Switzenberg, D.F.; Laycock, W.E. 1961. **Marten and fisher introductions**. Game Policy No. 29. Lansing, MI: Michigan Department of Conservation.

Weckwerth, R.P.; Wright, P.L. 1968. **Results of transplanting fishers in Montana**. Journal of Wildlife Management. 32: 977-980.

Williams, B.W. 2006. **Applications of genetic methods in furbearer management and ecology: case studies of fishers, American martens, and bobcats**. East Lansing, MI: Michigan State University. M.S. thesis.

Williams, C.M. 1947. **Marten in Colorado**. Colorado Conservation Comments. 10: 12-13.

Wisconsin Department of Natural Resources. 1986. **Pine marten recovery plan**. Madison, WI: Wisconsin Department of Natural Resources.

Wood, N.A.; Dice, L.R. 1924. **Records of the distribution of Michigan mammals**. Michigan Academy of Sciences, Arts and Letters. 3: 425-469.

Woodford, J.; Eloranta, C.; Rinaldi, T.; Kohn, B. 2005. **Inventory, status, and management needs of American marten in northeast Wisconsin**. 2005 Summ. Rep. Rhinelander, WI: Wisconsin Department of Natural Resources.

Zielinski, W.J.; Kucera, T.E.; Barrett, R.H. 1995. **The current distribution of fisher, *Martes pennanti*, in California**. California Fish and Game. 81: 104-112.

Williams, Bronwyn W.; Gilbert, Jonathan H.; Zollner, Patrick A. 2007. **Historical perspective on the reintroduction of the fisher and American marten in Michigan and Wisconsin.** Gen. Tech. Rep. NRS-5. Newtown Square, PA: U.S. Department of Agriculture, Forest Service, Northern Research Station. 29 p.

Management of mustelid species such as fishers and martens requires an understanding of the history of local populations. This is particularly true in areas where populations were extirpated and restored through reintroduction efforts. During the late 19th and 20th centuries, fishers (*Martes pennanti*) and American martens (*Martes americana*) were extirpated from much of their southern range, including Michigan and Wisconsin. Both species have been restored to varying degrees in these states following multiple reintroductions and translocations. We describe the status of the original populations and changes in their status over time, and include source locations, release sites, release and reintroduction dates, and demographic characteristics of released animals. This synthesis is crucial for evaluating the relative success of reintroductions in Michigan and Wisconsin, and, combined with knowledge of the current condition of these populations, can provide valuable guidance on the future management of these species. We also assess the reintroduction of fishers and martens in Michigan and Wisconsin and discuss strategies for successful reintroductions.

KEY WORDS: *Martes pennanti*, *Martes americana*, translocation